THE CHURCH
AND THE MAN

THE MACMILLAN COMPANY
NEW YORK · BOSTON · CHICAGO · DALLAS
ATLANTA · SAN FRANCISCO

MACMILLAN & CO., LIMITED
LONDON · BOMBAY · CALCUTTA
MELBOURNE

THE MACMILLAN CO. OF CANADA, LTD.
TORONTO

THE CHURCH
AND THE MAN

BY

DONALD HANKEY

Author of "A Student in Arms," etc.

WITH A FOREWORD BY
C. H. S. MATHEWS

New York
THE MACMILLAN COMPANY
1917

CONTENTS

IN MEMORIAM
DONALD HANKEY

Killed in action on the Somme, 12th October.
1916.

THE news that Donald Hankey had fallen in action brought to thousands of people who had never seen him — and the present writer was one of these — the kind of poignant sense of loss which is usually associated with the death of an intimate personal friend. It was not merely that one felt that the Church and the nation had lost yet another man of brilliant gifts, who could ill be spared. The real secret of this sense of personal loss lay in the rich humanity, the extraordinary sympathy, the understanding of all sorts of men, which his writing revealed. We can almost

apply to him the description, in one of the
most perfect of all his essays, of the relation
which came to exist between " The Beloved
Captain " and his men: —

"There was a bond of mutual confidence and
affection between us, which grew stronger and
stronger as the months passed."

We felt that we really grew to know him,
and we were sure that he knew us through and
through.   This wonderful insight into human
nature gave him the power to speak di-
rectly to the human heart.   That he was
no mean theologian was clear from the
fact that, though handicapped by having left
school at the age of sixteen for the R.M.
Academy at Woolwich, and having subsequently served for six years in the R.G.A.,
he secured a Second Class in Theology at
Oxford.   But his great aim, and his great
achievement in theology, was the interpretation in life of the learning of the schools.

He sought and he found a gospel for the plain man, educated or uneducated, which took into real account the progress of critical learning. A singularly inept reviewer, in a rationalist paper, gibed at him for saying in *Faith or Fear?*

" I learnt to reconcile Genesis and the *Origin of Species,* or rather to read the one without being worried by recollections of the other."

On this the reviewer in question triumphantly remarks : —

" Precisely! Put aside the facts of evolution, and it is quite easy to accept a theory of special creation the day before yesterday, or to mould that theory into a shape which its author could not recognize."

But of course Donald Hankey neither accepted nor moulded any " theory of special creation." He read the first chapters of Genesis, as every Modernist reads them, as the noblest of all creation-myths, and as far

more akin to poetry than to science. He
had nothing in common with those extraordi-
narily dull and stupid persons who produce
elaborate attempts to " reconcile " the letter
of scripture with the teaching of science. He
could not have anything in common with
them, for he was not stupid, and he never
wrote anything that was dull. But though
his singular honesty and candour made him
ready to recognize and accept whatever results of criticism seemed to him to be as-
sured, he himself was not, and he never pro-
fessed to be, a critic. He said of himself,
in his preface to his first book, *The Lord of
all Good Life* — quite the best book, by the
way, to put into the hands of the average
person seeking for a positive statement of
the truth of the Gospel, without ignoring or
explaining away real difficulties, in regard,
for instance, to miracles — that he " is not
concerned to temper the wind (of criticism)

to the shorn lamb," nor anxious to "reassure" any one. His object is just to set forth his own honestly thought out faith, and he closes this same preface with this characteristic sentence: —

"To the laity of the Church of England, to all who in shops, and factories, and barrack-rooms, and messes, and colleges, and hospitals, and ships, and wherever else men are gathered together, are trying to fight the battle of Christ with the poorest of equipment, this book is dedicated in loving fellowship."

There is no need here to repeat the story of his own inner life, since he has told it in his own words in the first chapters of this book, but it is perhaps worth while pointing out that, after he had lost the second-hand beliefs of his childhood, his progress towards a vital and evangelistic personal faith had four distinct phases. First, he came to see the impossibility of accounting for the existence of the human spirit from the rationalist standpoint. This led him to Theism. He could not stop there. A vivid, personal experience set him seeking for the personal knowledge of Christ. To achieve this he left the Army, and went to Oxford. Oxford, he says, taught him that it was possible to be a Christian without doing violence to his intellectual honesty, but it did not give him " a gospel for ordinary men," nor did he find this at Leeds Clergy School. But he could be content with nothing less, and he saw that in order to get it he must first know ordinary men. To gain this knowledge he embarked on the adventurous odyssey which really only ended with his death. On this odyssey he learnt the secret that only he can aspire to teach men who is always learning from them. In the Oxford settlement in Bermondsey, in the steerage of a German liner, in the Bush of Australia, in the barrack-room, and in hospital, he learnt to love his fellow-men, and to know them with the insight that is born of love. And in them he found the Christ for whom he sought. He found Him, as indeed the Gospel taught him to find Him, very often unrecognized by those who without knowing it served Him, and very often crucified by those who knew not what they did. And so it was that he read the Gospel in the light cast upon it by his insight into the hearts and the spiritual needs of " the common people," and then, in his first book, he set himself to re-interpret *The Lord of all Good Life* to the men he so passionately loved. He had found now the secret of all vital religious teaching, for he had learnt to read the ancient documents of the Faith in the light of the signs of his own times, and to interpret the signs of the times in the light of the ancient records. He " searched the scriptures " indeed, but, unlike the scribes and the pharisees, he remembered that from the religious point of view these were valueless except in so far as they led to the recognition of the living Saviour of men.

So he came to teach, like the Master whose loyal disciple he was, "with authority, and not as the scribes." And, as we all know, the war gave to him, just as he seemed to have mastered this secret, what he believed to be his great opportunity. "With the man in the street," he says, "it is not words that count, but deeds." He, who could have had a commission for the asking, humbled himself to enlist with "the common people," to share to the full the drudgery and hardship of the life of the camp and the trenches. He hated war with all his heart. He distrusted, as every sensitive soul must distrust, his own courage. "I am really not at all brave," he once wrote to me, and, in another letter, he described the war as "Hell — with compensations "— the compensations consisting for him mainly in fellowship with men he loved and admired. When he was invalided home from the front, he found his chief relief from the boredom of life in hospital, and, subsequently, in training (after he had accepted a commission, only because in view of the dearth of officers he felt it his duty to do so), by writing his wonderful articles in the *Spectator,* and his share of *Faith or Fear?* In the former, published in book form, with the title *A Student in Arms,* he just wrote of life in the new army as he knew it, and of his comrades and his officers as he knew them. It does not profess to be a religious book, but it is the most religious book yet written about the war. It has none of the ecclesiastical self-consciousness of such a book as *Priests in the Firing Line.* It is religious because, for Donald Hankey, all life was fundamentally religious. It was just this that made life so well worth living, and so well worth laying down in a good cause. For the chaplain this book is not merely a literary delight, it is a storehouse of materials for better sermons than he has ever preached to his men before. For Donald Hankey, Jesus Christ was really and truly "the Captain of our Salvation"— the Beloved Captain — who shares to the full the experiences of His men, asks them to do nothing He would not do Himself, and is with them at every moment, whatever their need may be. He really believed what many profess to believe without really believing it, that "of ourselves we can do no good thing." Therefore, wherever he found goodness he found God. He would never have assented to such an idea as that propounded by the Bishop of London in his preface to Canon Box's recent book, that the Virgin birth marks the difference between

One who is divine and one who would other-
wise have been "only a good man." For
him "if man is the son of nature he is also"
(just in so far as he is truly and fully man)
"the son of God, his Father in heaven."
As he says in the first Appendix to *The Lord
of all Good Life:* —

"It is only the fact that the Virgin Birth and the
bodily resurrection are told of Jesus that makes
them appear credible to those who believe in Jesus.
In other words, none can be asked to believe that
Jesus was the Son of God because He is said to have
been born of a virgin, and to have risen bodily from
the grave; though it may happen that a person who
believes, on other grounds, that Jesus was the Son
of God, and is now alive, may feel that the stories
of the virgin birth and the resurrection of the body
are for that reason either probably, or even necessarily, true. To them the story told by St. Luke
will be acceptable. That is to say that though these
stories are not evidence of the Divine Sonship of
Jesus, they may be regarded as implied by it. Since,
however, the Divine Sonship cannot be proved by
these stories, it follows that it cannot be disproved
by their rejection. It must also be pointed out that

the rejection of these stories does not discredit the remainder of the Gospels of which they are a part, because all higher critics are agreed that they are derived from different sources to the rest of the Gospels."

And he concludes this same appendix by saying: —

"The man who has recognized the freedom of Jesus and has found freedom and power in trying to imitate Him and share His point of view, and by praying in His Name to His Father, and who has found love and fellowship and life as a member of His Body the Church, will not easily doubt either that He was the Son of God, or that He is alive. The man who has not experienced any of these things, nor recognized them in others, has not understood the foundations of Christianity."

We have quoted this passage at length because, in its fearless honesty, in its consecrated common sense, it is quite typical of all Hankey's theological writing.

No theology which could not stand the test of life had any kind of validity for him.

It was a shock to him to find professing Christians unable to face the perils of the trenches and having to be sent back out of the danger zone. Christianity, for him, made men free, as His Master was free, from the tyranny of all external circumstances, and above all, from the tyranny of fear. And always he tested his theory in action. It was wholly characteristic of him that quite deliberately he set himself to discuss the truth about the fear of death. Did men fear death or not? If not, what did they fear? He concluded that most men had no fear of death when they were faced by it, though there was in them a natural physical shrinking from the indignity of wounds and mutilation and physical pain . . . and then having made his observations and written down his conclusions, he went out to test his theories in the thick of the fight. . . . He faced death as gallantly as he had faced life, and, true disciple of His Master as he was, he made of death not a defeat, but the final victory of his life.

C. H. S. MATTHEWS.

THE CHURCH AND THE MAN

THE CHURCH AND THE MAN

CHAPTER I

A PERSONAL EXPLANATION

THE object of these papers is to try to help find out how we can make the Church a better, a more efficient, a more vital, a more healthy body for Our Lord Jesus Christ. It is a subject which no one who loves the Master and reveres Him as the Son of God can approach without a feeling of the greatest diffidence, the most utter humility, the most searching self-criticism. For the member who has himself failed, as we have all failed, to criticize the failure of the body is a task from which any one may well shrink. Moreover, the reader will naturally want to know what sort of a person it is that is daring to criticize, what credentials he has. Therefore I have been asked to write a personal preface to my chapters, so as to give the reader some chance of forming an opinion as to what weight to attach to my ideas. No one likes to be accused of egoism, and it does seem egotistical to write about oneself; but the request seems so reasonable that I am going to take the risk, and try to comply with it.

In my boyhood I learnt to connect Churchmanship with all that was good and noble in life. My mother was a devout Churchwoman, and she was also a very humble, very unselfish woman, giving herself up completely to her husband, her children, and the poor and unfortunate among her neighbours. My father, though a layman, was a great reader of theology, and as a proof of his breadth of view I may mention that his favourite writers were Maurice, Robertson, Haweis, Dale, Westcott, and McLeod Campbell. I never learnt to connect religion with narrowness, or with smug self-satisfaction, or with harsh judgments of others, because these features were wholly absent from the religion of my home.

When I was sixteen I lost my mother, and went to the R.M. Academy, Woolwich, afterwards obtaining a commission in the Royal Garrison Artillery. In the six years which followed I learnt something of the average immorality of the unreligious man, which disgusted me, and of the scepticism that is embodied in the publications of the Rationalist Press Association. At last, when I was in a distant tropical colony, I found that I was on the brink of materialistic determinism. I hated it; but my belief in the Bible as the word of God had been shattered, and the pygmy insignificance of man considered as a

purely physical being had sunk into my soul.
Just as I had almost decided that the only
honest thing to do was to abandon all pre-
tence of religion, I had an experience which
revealed to me once for all that it was impossible for me to deny the reality of the human
soul, and the effective existence of men's conscience and reason and emotions.   I suddenly
realized that man was not only of pygmy insignificance by reason of his short life and
limited strength, but that he was also, by virtue of his unique self-consciousness, immeas-
urably greater than any purely physical or-
ganism.   He was at once an insect and a
god in comparison with the rest of the uni-
verse.   I can best sum up my thought in a
doggerel verse that I wrote at the time:—

> Am I an atom in a soulless scheme,
> My body real, but my soul a dream?
> Ah yes, ah yes, but how explain the birth
> Of dreams of soul upon a soulless earth?

I have never found another answer but that of Christ, that if man is the son of nature he is also the son of God, his Father in heaven.

From that day I was a theist. It was something, but not enough. A mere abstract belief that God exists is not of much practical use to any one. I longed for something more inspiring, and one day this sentence flashed across my mind: "If you would know Christ, behold He is at work in His vineyard." I took the vineyard to mean poorer England, and at the earliest opportunity I resigned my commission with a view to becoming a slum parson. I was advised to go to a university, and in due course went to Oxford and read the Honours school of theology. Oxford proved stimulating intellectually. I did not consort very much with what we irreverently designated "the Pi Push," feeling that I should learn more by making friends outside the circle of those who were intending to be ordained. I learnt to reconcile Genesis and the " Origin of Species," or rather to read the one without being worried by recollections of the other. I learnt to love the prophets and the epistles, and to find in the study of Comparative Religion a strong reason for believing in the especial inspiration of both Judaism and Christianity. I learnt to be intellectually a Modernist, and to find that I could be a Christian without doing violence to my intellectual honesty. But I did not learn a gospel for ordinary men. My religion was still mainly an intellectual matter, and not inspiration or power or love.

After a holiday in the wilds of Africa, and in Madagascar, I went to a clergy school, where I first saw parochial life at close quarters. What I saw alarmed me. I felt that I had no gospel for the working man, and that the life of a clergyman offered after all no prospect of usefulness to me. I funked it, and went instead to a Mission in poorer London. I went as a layman and not as a clergyman, as a learner rather than as a teacher.

It was there that I remembered the sentence which had come to my mind many years before. It was at the bedside of a boy dying of consumption that I felt for the first time that I had realized the presence of Christ, working in His vineyard. As time went on, however, I felt more and more that I could not preach to these working boys until I had in some way shared their life in a degree far greater than was possible as a manager of clubs. Everything was so easy for me and so hard for them that I simply could not preach to them without feeling a hypocrite. At the same time, it was obviously impossible to become a working man in England. At last I determined to try to become one in Australia, and took a passage in the steerage of a German liner. There I slept in a part of the hold which was fitted up to accommodate more than two hundred men. The men who slept above and below and round me were mostly Welsh miners, and in the following five weeks I learnt a good deal about human nature in the rough. On arriving in Australia I found it much harder than I had expected to become a working man. I worked in all for about six months in the bush, and learnt a little of what it means to do hard manual labour in pretty rough surroundings. At the same time, it was not quite what I had hoped for, and in the end the call of the fleshpots became too insistent, and I became a journalist roaming about Australia in search of copy.

After this half-success I returned to London, and again lived near the Mission, and helped to run a boys' club. My year of wandering had taught me a good deal, and I found myself able to write a book [1] which was an attempt to express in simple language and for simple people a Modernist Gospel. I was also allowed to prepare twelve boys from my club for Confirmation, an experience which I shall never forget, and which led to at least one freindship which I do not think will end.

Then came the war, and I enlisted in Kitchener's Army. I spent nine months in England and three at the front in the ranks, and feeling that I had learnt a little more I spent my time in hospital writing the first of the *Spectator* articles which have since been published under the title " A Student In Arms." Since then I have held a commission.

Looking back, I think that during my first years in the army I was learning disillusion-

---

[1] "The Lord of All Good Life." (Longmans. 2s. 6d.)

ment, the degradation of man under the influence of a pessimistic determinism. During the past five years I have been slowly
learning what appears to me a sane idealism,
and the wonderful potentialities of man for
unselfishness and courage and nobility when
he is under the influence of a sane and genu-
ine religious faith. I speak not of what I
have myself attained, but of what I have seen
in other men and women, more particularly
in those who have been faced with misfor-
tune and suffering. It is they who have
taught me more than any one else to believe
and to hope and to aspire. As I write now
I have absolutely no doubt of the power of
Christ to transform character and life, to
change the poor physical pygmies that we
men are into beloved sons of God and in-
heritors of life eternal. And that is why I
feel bound to do what I can to try to increase
the vitality and efficiency of Christ's body

the Church, that it may prove in the future a
more adequate medium for the exercise of
His wonderful power and love than it has
been in the past.

CHAPTER II

THE Average Man is not a Churchman. That is a statement that needs qualifying. Legally he is a Churchman — he has been baptized. Actually, however, he would not claim the title unless for census purposes, or on enlistment, he had to state definitely that he was something or nothing. He is not an Atheist. He has a religion of a sort. He feels that he is more " C. of E." than anything else. But he does not go to church. He does not pray. He does not believe the creeds. He does not attempt to regulate his life by the Church's moral law. To all intents and purposes he is not a Churchman.

He has a religion of a sort; but he would

be hard put to it if he had to explain what it was. His beliefs are unformulated. Even his code of morals and conduct generally is an unwritten one. We must try to formulate it for him. To do so is not easy. You can't deduce the average man's religion from his actions or character. Religion, when it is as nebulous as his, does not rule a man's life. The clue is rather to be found in the qualities which he admires, despises, or detests in other people. He has an ideal; but it is other people rather than himself that he judges by the standard of that ideal. Himself he does not judge — chiefly because he has never learnt to pray.

The Average Man admires courage, generosity, practical kindness, single-minded honesty, persistence in trying to do the right thing.

The Average Man despises meanness, physical fear, moral cowardice, instability, equivocation, narrow-mindedness, subservience to mere rank or wealth or power.

The Average Man hates "swank," cant, and cruelty.

These are the kind of things that the Average Man admires, despises, or hates. His ideal is a man who possesses all the qualities that he admires, and is free from all the defects that he despises or hates. Funnily enough, so far as it goes, his ideal is strangely like the ideal of the gospels. Moreover, it is the possession of this ideal that is the Average Man's religion, in so far as he has one; so that one would expect him to be some sort of a Christian. So he is, in a rather ineffective way. And he recognizes the fact by calling himself " C. of E." when he enlists.

But is the Average Man's ideal really much like the ideal of the gospels? He admires courage. Is courage a Christian virtue? Surely. The only fear that Christ countenanced was the fear of those who have power to kill the soul. The faith which Christ preached made fear an impossibility. The disciples feared the storm because they had not faith. Christ did not fear the storm. The disciples were afraid of the Pharisees, the Priests, Herod, public opinion; Jesus was not. He had faith; they had it not. The disciples were anxious about ways and means. They feared starvation and nakedness. Jesus did not. He had faith; they had it not. Jesus Christ feared absolutely nothing, because He had faith in the love and power of God the Father, and He felt certain that as long as He loved and obeyed His Father no real harm could happen to Him. The faith of Jesus was a perfect love of the good God, and perfect love casteth out fear. Courage is a fundamental Christian virtue. Fear is the first false god from whose power the gospel frees us.

Generosity and practical kindness — are these Christian virtues? It is hardly necessary to answer. Jesus was described as a man who " went about doing good." If the first law of the kingdom was to love God with all one's faculties, the second was to love one's neighbour as oneself. It is more blessed to give than to receive. Do to others as you would they should do unto you. Love your enemies — which means want to make them your friends; want them to alter, so that friendship between you may be possible; pray for that. Be willing to give anything — even your life. This is all in the gospels, as every one knows.

What about single-minded honesty? Let your yea be yea, and your nay, nay. Seek the kingdom, and let other things follow;

and seeking the kingdom means seeking for the things of God — justice, mercy, love, truth. Dishonesty and equivocation are always the fruit either of fear or of selfishness. The man who has the courage of faith and who loves his neighbour as himself will never be guilty of either.

Persistence? Be not weary in well-doing. Instability is incompatible with either real faith or real love.

Was ever any one less narrow-minded than Christ? He feasted with publicans and sinners. He healed lepers. He forgave harlots. He foretold the conversion of the Gentiles. He ridiculed narrow laws and prejudices at every turn. You cannot be narrow if you have once known and loved the Heavenly Father.

As for " swank " and cant, and snobbish subservience to rank and wealth, they were the very things that Christ loathed and fought

against most of all. When the disciples
boasted, He set a child in their midst, as an
example of humility. He told the Pharisees
that their self-satisfied righteousness was
nothing but cant, and that it set them far
further from the kingdom of heaven than
any amount of downright sin.

No, there is not a single feature of the
Average Man's ideal which is not part and
parcel of the ideal which Jesus Christ taught
and embodied. And once you have understood His point of view, His sense of perspec-
tive, all these features are seen to be necessary, inevitable, and comprehensible. Once
realize the greatness of God, as Christ realized and taught it, and the littleness of man
follows. Once realize the fatherly love of
God, as Christ realized and taught it, and
the greatness of man follows — his real
greatness. And from that vision of the
greatness and the love of God all courage and

love towards men, and humility, and honesty, and independence follow with irrefutable logic.

Now, you Average Man, how is it that, since Christ fulfils and embodies and explains your ideal, you are not enrolled under His banner? Why not range yourself under the standard of the Cross with the rest who are trying to embody Him?

"Why quarrel about a name," you say, "if I am following the same ideal? Did not Christ Himself say, 'He that is not against us is for us'?"

But what I complain about is that though you have an ideal you don't make any real attempt to follow it out. Don't you realize that your talk of courage is all humbug, and that you are actually living the life of a toady — a toady to convention and class prejudice and public opinion? Don't you realize that your talk of generosity is all cant, and that you are actually living the most selfish life imaginable, thinking of nothing so much as of your own comfort and position and reputation? Don't you realize the cruelty of your profit-mongering and your immorality? Don't you see that your pleasures are bestial, and that your morals are dragging down the whole race? Pull yourself together. If you believe in your ideal, for goodness sake try to follow it out. What? You don't want to " set up to be good"? You know you can't succeed, do you? What's that? However much you try, death and fate will mock you in the end? Ah, my friend, what you need is religion, after all. It is no good having an ideal unless you are an optimist, and you can't be a rational optimist without believing in God. You can't believe in God? Why, man, the very fact that you can't make a decent fist of life without this belief in God, this rational basis of optimism, is surely a sufficient proof of its truth!

You don't see that you are any worse than the average Churchman, and you don't see that going to church is going to bring you any nearer to your ideal? That is the point, is it? Do you believe in Christ? Yes. Do you believe in the Church which is His body? No. Well, then, join the Church so that you may be in a position to improve it!

You won't? I know one reason, O average man! You are human, you have passions, you have given way to them, and you don't believe in your ability to conquer them. Yet stay and consider. In Christianity marriage is a holy thing — the consecration to God's service of God's greatest gift to men, the power of creation: a holy partnership in which the Great Giver of Life is a third. Is not that your ideal, too? Don't you agree that you would be better and happier if you tried to live up to it?   If so, it is up to you to try to live up to your ideal, and to be pure up till marriage so that your marriage may be really holy.   It is a poor thing to have an ideal and not to try to live up to it; and, mind you, this is all that Christ asks of you — to go on trying hopefully. You very likely can't succeed right away, but if you go on trying hopefully, and genuinely hating your failure, you are a Christian.

CHAPTER III

THE TROUBLES OF AN AVERAGE LAYMAN

An Average Man came to the conclusion that it was up to him to become a Churchman. Jesus Christ was his ideal after all. If he could embody even a little bit of Jesus, that was good enough. So he came to Communion and found in the breaking of bread and in the drinking of the wine the symbols of the very essence of his faith. He knelt and said, "Lord Jesus, I want to be a bit of Thee. I want to show a little bit of Thee to the world. I want to offer Thee my body to be a member of Thy Body, that it may show to the world a little of Thy Spirit. O Lord Jesus, it is a wretched thing that I offer Thee. Yet Thou canst use it if Thou

wilt, and purify it for Thy purpose." And
the Lord Jesus gave to him bread and wine,
and said, " Dear brother, thy gift I accept.
So long as thou offerest it, I will receive it,
and will live again in the world in thee and
in thy brethren. Take this bread, it is My
token that thou art a member of My body.
Take this wine. It is the token that while
thou offerest thyself to Me, My Spirit shall
live in thee, and show itself to the world."
And to all that were assembled there the
Lord said, " By this shall all men know that
ye are My disciples, if ye have love one to
another." And they all went their ways, and
did not meet till the following Sunday.

The Average Man had become a layman,
and he was at once profoundly happy, and
profoundly discontented. On the one hand
he was clear about his ideal. He was trying to follow it, and finding an altogether un-
expected joy in doing so. On the other

hand, he did not find in the visible and organized Church that fellowship, that straight-
forward simplicity, that sure help, which he
had been led to expect.

At the very start he had been discouraged.
It was found that after all he had never been
baptized. At first he was rather glad of
this. He said as much to the parson.

"Padre," said he. "I'm glad of this.
It's a chance to get things square. I want to
be quite clear about the proposition that I
am taking up. I want to stand up before you
and my witnesses, and to say quite plainly
to them that I want to fight beneath the
Cross, the standard of Jesus Christ; that I
want to be a member of His body, and to do
my bit towards showing Him to the world.
I want to say that I don't believe in selfishness
and material ambition, and that I do believe
in goodness, and honesty, and love, and
freedom."

" M'yes," said the parson. " We shall have to use the service for the baptism of such as be of riper years."

" What's that? " asked the Average Man in alarm.

" Here it is," said the parson, handing him a prayer-book open at the place.

The Average Man began to read it.

" I say," he protested. " Why drag in Noah and the Red Sea? I don't think I quite believe in them, you know! "

" That's all right," said the padre. " You haven't got to."

" Well, but can't you leave them out? It seems to make the thing unreal somehow."

The Average Man read on.

" I say," he said again. " This is awfully long-winded. What exactly do you mean by ' mystical washing away,' ' spiritual regeneration,' ' elect children,' ' everlasting salvation,' and being ' damned '? "

" Don't you worry about that," said the parson. " The service is an old one. I am satisfied that you have got the main points right, and that is all that matters."

" But can't you cut them out? And look here, do you steadfastly believe that Christ was born of the *Virgin* Mary, and that He *went down* into Hell, and *ascended* into Heaven, and that He will come to judge the *quick* and the dead? And do you really believe in the resurrection of the *flesh*, because I am hanged if I do?"

" The Church has always affirmed that the Christ was born of a virgin," said the padre, " though I don't really feel strongly about this point of doctrine. As for going down and ascending I think that essentially I mean the same as the writer of the creed, though I should put it differently. As for the second coming in the lifetime of the world, I believe in it as a possibility rather than as a certainty.   I certainly believe in the survival of personality, which is the only important thing about the ' resurrection of the flesh.' "

" That's all very well," objected the Average Man, " but here am I, at the most important moment of my life, when I am trying to make a clean start in a new sort of life altogether, and I have got to make a public and solemn confession of faith with all sorts of mental reservations.   I don't like it.   Why can't I say straight out what you and I really do believe? "

" You've got to obey the rules, that's all," said the padre.   " And they aren't up to date."

" Well, I suppose I must equivocate a little to obtain so great a fellowship," said the Average Man.   " But I must say, I wish it wasn't necessary."

And as time went on he kept on running

up against the same difficulty. The Church services, instead of being a help to him, continually worried him by their apparent irrelevance and insincerity. The preaching that he heard generally seemed off the point too. The choir worried him; because it " rendered " the service in a way which made it impossible for him to join in, and because he knew that it consisted of choirmen who were only interested in the musical aspect of the service, and of boys who weren't interested at all. He felt that one ought not to have to pay men to praise God for one. But what worried him more than anything was that he had no friends among the congregation. He felt that this was absolutely wrong, and that as fellow members of Christ's body they ought to be united. All men should know that they were His disciples by the fact that they loved one another. Yet most of them he simply could not love. He knew them as reputable men; but they were men who kept themselves to themselves, priding themselves on their respectability in a manner which seemed almost Pharisaical. One or two of them he knew were hard employers, who made a living by paying their men as little as possible, and working them as hard as possible. The communion of saints seemed to be lacking. The corporate embodiment of the Lord Jesus seemed to be in abeyance. Such keenness as did exist seemed to centre round certain committees and meetings, where little matters of procedure and ritual, which seemed to the Average Man of infinite unimportance, were debated with great heat.

And all the time he did need the fellowship of his brethren so badly. For he soon found that, however much he might like his comrades who were not Churchmen, there was now a gulf between them. The average joke was a joke that he simply could not laugh at and be loyal to his Master. The average amusement was such that he simply could not go to it. These jokes and amusements were not clean. They were poisonous. They degraded man and woman to the level of the beast, and he had determined to regard them as the children of God. So he found himself not disliked, not persecuted, but just left out, and that by his own will. It was hard. He was no longer the Average Man, and at times he almost wished he were. Being a Churchman did not make him feel self-righteous. He knew that God had called him to follow a higher ideal than the rest, and that he was to be judged henceforth by a higher standard; and while he thanked God for that high calling, at times he felt terribly lonely and sore in need of help.

The Church had endued him with a new hunger; but it failed to satisfy it.

CHAPTER IV

THE GOSPEL AND THE CHURCH

THE fact is that the gospel for the individual is a simple matter to understand, while the Church is a very complicated affair. The layman in the last chapter had no difficulty in understanding the practical meaning of the profession that he had undertaken. It was simply that he had to try to look at everything from a new point of view, the point of view of Jesus Christ, a point of view from which the greatness of God filled the landscape, while the individual disappeared into insignificance except in so far as he stood out in the light of God's love. So things temporal suddenly became very unimportant, while things eternal loomed large. The effect of this point of view on the man who had assimilated it could be easily foretold. In proportion as the assimilation was complete he would approach more nearly to the ideal which is the ideal of every wholesome man, and which was the ideal taught and exemplified by Christ. For the individual, we repeat, the gospel is plain enough. It is simply the imitation of Christ, and there is no real doubt about the manner of man that Christ was.

But the Church is concerned with a host of other questions, which so occupy it that there is hardly any time left for the gospel. The Church is busy with literary and historical criticism, comparative religion and anthropology, cosmogony, embryology, psychology, metaphysics, apostolic succession, symbolic theology, mediævalism, modernism, ritualism, protestantism, preservation of continuity, adaptation to modern needs, rela-

tions with the State, finance, socialism, re-
union, organized philanthropy, foreign missions, and countless other questions of ap-
parently vital and pressing importance.
Moreover, the Church is " all of a muddle."
It can't see its way through. It is rent at
every turn by violent antagonisms within the
fold. On every question men are calling
each other " obscurantists," " traitors,"
" heretics," " schismatics," " Laodiceans,"
" fanatics," and so on. It is very certain that
in this, as in other ages of the history of the
Church, outsiders would be puzzled to recognize the disciples of Christ by the love that
they bear towards one another.

Something is wrong, and an ever-increas-
ing number of men and women within the
Church are feeling that all this strife and
controversy is beside the point; that in it the
gospel is lost sight of; that what we want
to do is just to drop all these questions, and

to get back to the main point, which is, after all, to embody Christ. We know that some people will go on wrangling, but why should every simple child that comes to school to learn how to be a child of God be dragged into the controversy? Why should every simple workman who comes to Church to worship God be involved in these unprofitable complications? There is no getting out of it, they are involved. Every child who is taught the Book of Genesis as part of his religious education is predestined to an eventual plunge into the murky waters of controversy. Every workman who comes to Church and sings the present psalter and listens to the present lectionary and repeats the present creeds is going to have his faith complicated by some of these unnecessary and unedifying wrangles.

What are we to do — we who only want to get the main issue plain? We are con-

fronted by three alternatives. The first is
to initiate a campaign for the reformation
of the Church and the revision of its methods and textbooks in the interests of simplicity and of the coming of the kingdom.
That means that we plunge into the sea of
controversy, and try to obtain the mastery.
Could we but have a free hand we are sure
that we could reform the Church! Ah yes;
but so are all our brother zealots of the op-
posing camps. They are all in earnest.
They are all sure that they are right. All
that any of them wants is a free hand. I
confess that in former days I have pinned
my faith to such a campaign; but lately I
have begun to doubt whether any godly result can issue from this fratricidal strife.
Moreover, we are, after all, only a section of
the Church. Let us be humble enough to
admit that if we had a free hand in revising
the Church of today, a new generation would

demand to revise our revision twenty years hence. I think that it is really almost necessary that the Church should be something of a compromise, and somewhat behind the times.

The second alternative is to cut ourselves off from the Church, and its strife and corruption, and to start a new Church of our own, which shall be pure and holy indeed. Alack, my brethren, how many have done this very thing in the last hundred years, and, with what result? Why, narrowness, poverty of life and pride, till they too have become corrupt and moribund. No, brethren, the life of Christ is in His body the Church, for all its infidelity. We cannot make Him a new body, other than that which He has chosen, for His Spirit will not dwell therein.

The third alternative seems to me to be the right one, and it is to take full advantage of the liberty that is allowed within the

Church. I have in mind a little settlement in one of our great cities, where a few university men and many men of the place have grown into a brotherhood which is, as it seems to me, very real, very Christian, very pure in its ideals, very simple in its teaching and worship and manner of life, and which combines a very real unity with the English Church with a very real freedom from unnecessary complications. The premises of the settlement consist of a central house, where the secretary and a house-keeper live. The house contains a common-room, diningroom, chapel, and bath-room which are free to all members of the committee of the men's clubs, and the " officers " of the boys' clubs. Besides this house there are two men's clubs and four boys' clubs. The constitution is extremely democratic, and remarkably elastic in every way. Short prayers close each club every evening. On Sunday there is a simple and elastic service in each boys' club, and an equally simple service in Church for the men. Once a month there is corporate Communion in the church, followed by a simple breakfast taken in common, and paid for by those who attend. Every Sunday evening there is a quite indescribable service in the chapel for the "officers" and communicants, which alternates according to circumstances between a Bible class, a prayer meeting, and a fellowship of silence, and is always a mixture of the three. By agreement with the rector of the parish the candidates for Confirmation are prepared under arrangements made by the "warden," who is always a layman, and seldom a professional theologian. Of course I am describing pre-war days. The result was, in my opinion, quite extraordinary. The brotherhood was continually faced with crises, such as the loss of its indispensable members; yet in the event no one was found to be indispensable. Members have been scattered broadcast over the world, yet I know of hardly one who has forgotten, or who, having once been a communicant, has since ceased to be one. When the war came it seemed as if the brotherhood would have to be for the time disbanded, yet it is, so far as the junior clubs are concerned, more flourishing than ever, though almost without *personnel* to manage it; while a monthly news and correspondence sheet shows that there is hardly a member who does not feel that absence has even strengthened the invisible bond that unites him to his brethren and his spiritual home.

This is just one example of the way in which in loyalty to the English Church a free society may grow up and flourish, and with the benediction of bishop and rector unite men in a simple faith such as is almost impossible in the ordinary official parochial organization.   By means of such groups within the Church, ideals may be pursued and developed and justified without schism or disloyalty, without the danger of narrowness that comes from complete separation.   By remaining within the fold they both nourish and are nourished by the Church, without losing any reasonable degree of freedom. Further, it is remarkable that in the particular instance described above the relations between the brotherhood and the official Church have steadily grown in cordiality. Suspicion, which was rife at first, has died.

It is, I am convinced, by using the freedom of the Church to pursue our ideals that we shall both avoid the pitfalls of separatism and commend our ideas to the Church. It is not by talking, but by being and doing that truth is made known, and purged of error.   Had Jesus Christ been but a prophet there would have been no Christian Church

today.   It is because He was the Son, and
because He lived and died perfectly, that
He is our Lord and Master now.   And so
with His disciples, it is not by controversy or
organization, but by holy living and holy
dying that they will purify His Church, and
fill the world with the knowledge of God.

CHAPTER V

METHODS AND WEAPONS

SUPPOSING that a new movement did spring up within the Church, and that men and women who felt that they were clear about the main issue did form groups within the Church where they could work for their ideals with loyalty and reasonable freedom, what should be their methods and weapons? To begin with, it is probably essential that the movement should *not* be organized or centralized. At the present juncture centralization would mean controversy and loss of freedom. We want to keep out the people who have a passion for regulation and diplomacy. We want plain humble effort, with any amount of variety and experiment.

We don't want notoriety or advertisement. We don't want to be labelled. We don't want to be dragged into the regions of criticism and controversy. We want to be the leaven that works unseen.

In the matter of worship and life and relations with the parish church, there must necessarily be infinite elasticity, to correspond with an infinite variety of conditions. In the matter of teaching, if we confine ourselves to the practical issue there will be little temptation to divergence. The gospel in its practical bearings is plain enough. All that we do want is a literature. This literature must not be prepared or issued by authority. That would immediately arouse suspicions and drag us into the arena of controversy. In character the essentials are that it should be positive and simple. Too much time and energy have already been spent in attacking what is false. What is now needed is the promulgation of what is true. And the ultimate test of truth for the ordinary man is experiment. Anything that can be tested by experiment is vital. Anything that cannot be tested by experiment can be left on one side. Was Christ born of a virgin? We cannot test that by experiment, and therefore it is not vital to the ordinary man. Leave it to the Church. Is Christ alive? That is a matter that can be tested. It is vital. Assume Him to be alive, and see whether it works. Does He really live in us if we offer Him our bodies for His dwelling place? Try to see. This is vital. Is love really stronger than fear? Is it really true that humility and unselfishness are more important than wealth and power? Is it true that life is eternal? Assume these propositions true, and if in doing so you find a new happiness and peace yours, the balance of probability is in their favour.   And if other men and women see that the fruits of your life are good, they will come and ask you to teach them too how to be happy and useful.

This is the new apologetic, which is as old as Christianity.   Not controversy but demonstration, not logic but power.   In the long run it is the only apologetic that counts.

But in talking of literature, what of the Bible?   There again the same test must be applied.   We want as much of the Bible as can help us practically.   We don't want any of the stuffing, or of the parts that are going to land us in controversy.   We want a shortened Bible for the use of plain people, and sooner or later some one will have to take this task in hand.   Probably there will be many experiments in this direction.   Parts of the Bible which are of infinite value to the educated man are quite useless to the workman or the child.   But in the Bible is the kernel of the faith, and we have got to dig it out and make it easy of access to all who need it.

There is one other way in which in some places it might be possible for us to help the Church. There is little doubt that one of the chief difficulties of the Church lies in the traditional status of the clergy. The parson's job is such that it does not bring him into very close touch with the ordinary laymen of his parish. Very often they fail to understand each other. It has been suggested in a certain parish that one or two laymen who have long worked in the parish in a more or less independent fashion should cement the union between their work and that of the parish church by becoming deacons for Sunday duty, while still continuing to earn their livings during the week by their civilian occupations. Such men, it is thought, would be a valuable link between the clergy and the laity, and the experiment might be worth trying in some places.

Above all, we must not aim at finality. This movement of which we have spoken may develop, it may be maturing even now, it may never begin; but if it does mature, it must be content to be like leaven, working unseen, and ready and glad to be absorbed more and more into the life of the whole. Unlike a separatist movement, it must aim at rendering itself unnecessary, its ultimate object must be its own disappearance.

CHAPTER VI

THE word " faith " is made to cover a
great deal of timidity and a great deal of
laziness. Young people who ask questions
about theology are told that they must re-
frain, and accept by an exercise of " faith "
what they cannot hope to understand. That
is one reason why young people who have
had " a Christian education " so seldom know
anything about Christianity. There are a
great many doctrines which are not only
highly agreeable to common sense, and easily understood, but are of absolutely vital
practical importance, and yet hardly any one
attempts to understand them because they
have always been taught to accept them in

" faith " instead of asking questions about them.

To begin with, the question of whether there is a God or not, is one which Christian teachers are often very unwilling to discuss. They feel that intellectually the case for the existence of God is a weak one. They say that there is only one thing to do, and that is to make an effort of faith and believe it. Consequently lots of people go away with the idea that it does not really matter very much whether they believe that God exists or not, as long as they try to " play the game." Yet really the question is one which should be absolutely of vital moment to every man. If there is a God he must look at life in one way, and if there is not he must look at it in another. His whole attitude towards life should vary according to the answer that he gives to this question. For if there is a God the evidence for His exist-

ence is found, not in antiquity, but in the
present-day man. The real question is,
" What is man? " If a man really has reason and will-power and conscience — all the
qualities which appear to distinguish him
from the mere creature of impulse and instinct — then they must have come from
somewhere. They must either be latent in
nature, or they must have come from some
Being outside of nature who possesses them.
In other words, either nature must have a
divine origin, or man must be the child, not
only of nature his mother, but also of God
His father. In either case God exists. But
if man's reason and conscience and will-
power are not real; if they have no effective
existence; if they are, as has been said, no
more than the by-products of a blind, insen-
state, conscienceless process, bearing much the
same relation to that process that the whir-
ring sound of the wheels of a piece of ma-

chinery bears to the machinery, having as little significance, and as little practical effect, then there is probably no God. The fact is that if a man is determined to take his will and reason and conscience seriously, he is implicitly assenting to the proposition that God exists, while if he decides to adopt a flippant, pessimistic, sceptical, invertebrate, jelly-fish sort of attitude towards life, he is implicitly denying the existence of God. Unless there is a God, goodness and generosity and nobility and heroism are mere names without any real meaning. They are dreams, vanity, nonsense. Few men will be willing to regard them as such, for to do so is to deprive life of all its interest and meaning. The theory of psychology which does not give a meaning to life as we have to live it is not likely to commend itself to us as likely to be true, however academically logical it may be.

Equally, the doctrine of the incarnation is agreeable to common sense. We human beings may be " spiritual," but it is quite impossible for us to understand or perceive the spiritual unless we can establish contact with it through the medium of our physical senses. Just as we see electricity revealed in its effects on matter, though the stuff itself eludes our senses, so we can only understand and perceive the divine Spirit in so far as He is revealed in His effects on physical beings. It is, we have argued, in man, the most highly developed of Nature's children, that we see the only clear and convincing evidence of the existence of the spiritual and of God. So too it is in man, and in the most perfect of men, that we shall see the fullest revelation of God, if we see Him at all. In fact, the most perfect man is necessarily the fullest revelation of God that we could possibly understand. By His freedom from all the fears and meannesses that degrade other men, by His peerless spiritual liberty, we acclaim the Christ as that most perfect Man, that fullest possible revelation of God in the only terms that we mortals can understand.

So, again, the " mystical union " between Christ and His Church is not nearly so hard to understand as the difficult words make one think.   If men are still to know God revealed in Christ, Christ must have a body through which to reveal Himself to men.   We can only know other men through their self-expression in their bodies, and we can only know Christ through His self-expression in a body.   But there is no man living who can show His wonderfully many-sided freedom and power to men.   Yet each can show some part of Him.   So, each showing a part, the Church corporate should show the whole, if the different members are really united in spirit.

Again, in the same way the mystery of Holy Communion becomes clear. We offer our bodies to Christ, that He may take them and show in each some part of Himself; and the bread and wine are the age-long pledge that what we offer He accepts. We pledge ourselves to be loyal to Him and to one another, and to combine to show the spirit of Christ to the world. So explained, the service of Holy Communion is clearly seen to contain the very epitome of our Christian faith and hope and duty. It is there at the altar that we perceive, most plainly and succinctly set forth, just what it means to try to be a Christian, and just where we are to look for help. Yet how many candidates for Confirmation fail to understand that Holy Communion is anything but a " Holy Mystery," incomprehensible and almost magical!

Priestly absolution, again, is very rational when it is properly understood, and very comforting too. Yet there are many who honestly believe that we hold the almost blasphemous doctrine that without the pronouncement of absolution by the priest, God does not forgive! What is the truth? Why, simply that Christ declared that as soon as a sinner repented and tried to amend, God forgave him. Christ announced this as a fact, and because men trusted that Christ was the Son of God they believed Him, and took advantage of God's forgiveness. Christ still proclaims this fact through His new Body the Church, and the members of that Body whose function it is to make that declaration in His name are the priests.

Even the mystery of the Holy Trinity is not repugnant to reason nor wholly incomprehensible if it is explained historically. As a fact of history, the first Christians stated that they believed in the Father and in the Son and in the Holy Spirit. Why?

Because of their experience. Peter first learnt the love of the Father through knowing the Son; but it was not till the Holy Spirit entered him and transformed him that the coward became infinitely brave, and the ambitious follower of the Messiah became the self-forgetful apostle of the gospel of salvation. Peter believed in one God; but he had known Him through two revelations, the revelation in Jesus Christ, and the revelation in his own transformation of character. So nothing would satisfy Peter's disciples but a belief in one God and in the three Persons who were the revelation of that God. The doctrine of the Holy Trinity was the creation, not of a subtle, philosophic mind, but of plain men who had had a certain experience, and who refused to accept any explanation of that experience which did not fit in with and allow for the facts as they had known them.

Over and over again one finds that the
Church in her teaching is lacking in simplicity, in the courage to try to understand
her heritage, in the realization that her doctrines that have been handed down from the
earliest days are not mere arbitrary and
mysterious revelations to be accepted with
an irrational and uncomprehending assent,
but doctrines pregnant with vital meaning
for life, and destined to revolutionize the
whole outlook and character of the man who
tries to understand and believe and apply
them.

It is very much the same with the Christian ethic. Only too often the practical
words of Christ, which were meant to de-
fine for us our attitude towards our fellow
men, are dismissed as a kind of idealism only
meant for a better world; and this is often
simply because the teachers of the Church
have not the courage to apply common sense

to their interpretation of these sayings. When Christ said, "Love your enemies," He meant it literally. He did not mean, "slobber over them." He did not mean, "condone their evil deeds." But He did mean, "wish them to be your friends." Christ loved the Pharisees as individuals, not for what they were, but for what they might be. He showed His love, not by shutting His eyes to their hypocrisy and pride, not by calling them "dear brothers," but by doing all He could to make them dissatisfied with themselves, so that they might become different, and so that they might become His friends. So we should love the Germans, not by letting them do evil and shutting our eyes to it, not by being blind to their hideous cruelty and lust for power; but by doing all we can to alter their attitude. Love must be wise. After the war we must be ready to be generous at the right moment; but it were a very mistaken love to forget, even where one is ready to forgive. Even God does not forgive the impenitent sinner. To do so were to condone his crimes.

Again, consider that other vexed question, the question of the sexual union of men and women. How often Christ's words are regarded as a mere arbitrary commandment, and how seldom does any one apply his common sense to interpret them. Yet Christ's point of view is easy to understand. " What God hath joined together, let no man put asunder." "He that looketh on a woman to lust after her hath committed adultery with her already in his heart." Sexual love among animals may well be a matter of physical instinct, for the resulting beings are beings which shall be guided by instinct. But the children of men and women are not children of nature, guided solely by physical instinct. They are, according to Christ, potential children of God. Therefore a man and woman must regard their marriage as a holy thing, for which they are responsible to God, since they are to bring into the world children for Him as well as for themselves.

The crying need at present is for the Church to realize the reasonableness and the simplicity of her gospel, and not to be afraid of explaining it to boys and girls and men and women in a simple and practical way. We want fewer long words, less philosophy, less mystery, more simple statement of vital and practical truth.

CHAPTER VII

THE CHURCH AND HUMAN RELATIONS

DOCTRINES, creeds, rites, ceremonies, constitution, discipline, all these are vain if the Church does not teach and show to the world the new life. "Though I speak with the tongues of men and of angels . . . though I have the gift of prophecy and know all mysteries and all knowledge, and though I give all my goods to feed the poor and my body to be burned, and have not love, I am nothing." In the long run the most disastrous failure of the Church is the failure to love. It is that which does more than anything else to alienate the man of good will. When he finds in the Church the spirit of exclusiveness, the spirit that sets store by class distinctions, and class prejudices, the spirit of self-satisfied aloofness from the troubles of the unfortunate, then he condemns the Church, not for her Christianity, but for her lack of it. And he is entitled to do so. Did not the Master say, " By this shall all men know that ye are my disciples, if ye have love one to another ".

Let us be frank. In spite of the multitude of her alms, the wide-spread net of her " charity," the Church is lacking in love. Church people are apt to thank God that they are not as other men. The man or woman who has poor garments is not made to feel that in the house of God, at any rate, he or she is welcomed as an honoured guest, which is undoubtedly how Jesus Christ would wish such to be welcomed. " I cannot go to church because I have no clothes," says the poor woman. " I have given up going to Communion till I can get a new suit. The people stared so," said an emigrant in an Australian mining town. " I didn't go to church because I was always put in the back seats, and didn't seem to be welcome," said a poor man who had shown wonderful faith during a long and painful illness. " Suitable accommodation is reserved for the poor of the parish," ran the legend in a large country church. " I wouldn't go to church if I had nasty smelly people next to me," said a lady church-goer. Such things should make us blush for very shame.

We have got to face this question of the Church and social distinctions. We have got to settle this question of human values. It is not going to be easy. It is not going to be a matter of gush. No amount of mere talk about " brotherhood " is going to slur over the existence and the recognition within the Church of a sort of pride that is about as definitely unchristian as anything well could be. Further, we are not going to solve this question by denying distinctions which obviously do exist, and by proclaiming an equality which obviously does not exist. Our brotherly love has got to be a practical thing which will take count of facts.

It is perfectly true that some men are better educated, have better taste, finer instincts than others. It is perfectly true that some men are better fitted to teach or to govern or to direct than others. It is perfectly true that in the life of Church and nation there must be authority and discipline. It is useless to deny these very patent facts. It is also quite evident that it is not within the power of the Church to decide whether the privileges of education and responsibility are to be hereditary or not. The Church has to deal with the social structure that has been evolved by the nation, and to make the best of it. It is not the business of the Church to identify herself with definite political movements. Individual Churchmen may properly do so. The Church as such may not.

On the other hand, the Church is not being true to her Master unless she can show how the social structure can be permeated with real unity and real love. If it is not possible for master and man, employer and employed, landlord and tenant, officer and soldier, to be united in Christ's fellowship of love, then the Church cannot be true to her ideals, Christianity is unpractical and impracticable. We had better give it up. If, on the other hand, Christianity gives us a point of view from which it is possible to recognize both distinctions and the brotherhood of man, the Church must try to show an example of how this double recognition can be effected. St. Paul tries to show us how he thinks this can be done. We are all members of one Body

— the Body of Christ; but every member has not the same function. The foot is not the hand, nor the hand the eye. There are diversities of gifts; but there should be the same Spirit. Each member has his particular gifts and his particular functions. All are necessary. All are interdependent. To the full working of the Body the efficiency of every member is essential. No one member can suffer without all the others suffering. None are to be despised. All are to be honoured, for all are indispensable. Indeed, very often it is just the member which is least attractive, least " comely," whose efficiency is most important.

Here is the basis of sound democracy — sane mutual respect. We cannot all be managers, foremen, officers, masters. The master without the man is as useless as the man without the master. At the very start it is necessary that they must respect each other, and recognize that the other's function is a necessary and therefore an honourable one.   We must get it out of our heads that manual labour, dirty labour, labour involving obedience to orders, are degrading. No labour is degrading.   All honest, necessary, useful labour is honourable.   The clean hands and tidy clothes of the clerk or the shop assistant do not constitute him a superior person to the navvy with his hard rough hands and his muddy breeches.   Nor do the strong muscles and tanned skin of the navvy constitute him a superior person to the pale and puny clerk.   In so far as each is doing necessary and useful work each should respect the other.   They belong to different classes.   It is inevitable that, as a rule, each should find his most congenial friends among those who follow his own manner of life.   It is inevitable that each should have his own way of spending his leisure.   It is inevitable that they should eat different food, drink different liquids, and wear different clothes. But they should not despise one another. Above all, they should not forget that they are sons of one Father, servants of one Master, temples of one Spirit, members of one Body, and that each is necessary to the other in the building up of that Body.

All this is such platitude that it seems hardly worth writing down, and yet when one comes to think of it our national life is simply made up of individual pride and mutual contempt. Each little section of society sets store by the distinctions in appearance and manner and intonation and way of living that divide it off from others. Each little section fights for its own political interest, completely oblivious of the interests of those other sections whose well-being is none the less intimately bound up with its own. Each little section prides itself on keeping itself to itself

on every possible opportunity and in every
department of life.   Men impose limitations
on themselves, conventions and prejudices
that narrow their sympathies, hamper their
generous instincts, destroy their freedom; and
then they hug to themselves those limitations,
glory in their self-forged chains.   Jim and
Jack may be friends at school.   They may
worship at the same church.   They may be
kindred spirits; but if Jack works with his
coat off and Jim with his on, if Jack has a
large family and has to live in a poor neigh-
bourhood while Jim has no family and lives in
a suburb, they will no longer be seen together.
In this matter women are even worse than
men.   A man while he is single may make
what friends he likes, and keep what friends
he likes.   He may live and give his affections
in freedom.   But let him marry and he is
immediately pigeon-holed, labelled with a

class, and henceforward he must not stray beyond that pigeon-hole.

Class distinctions as we honour them and as the Church recognizes them are a form of slavery. They limit freedom. They check natural impulses and affections. They promote jealousy and pride and strife. Christ offers us liberty, and commands us to love.

The foundation of Christian liberty, in this matter as in every other, is simply the vision of God. Once realize how far God is removed from man, and realize how His Love has bridged that gulf, and then all the petty pride and jealousy of human distinctions vanish from sight. If when men and women knelt or (for fear of bagging the knees of their trousers) bowed their heads in church, they realized that they were approaching the Infinite and Eternal, they could not go on priding themselves on the petty distinctions

of class, the soft white hands, the well-fitting
clothes, the clean, starched collars, and well-
brushed hair.   Their sense of humour would
set them free.   But there is no real worship
in our services.   There is no sense of proportion in our prayers.   God forgive us, we
have no eyes, no ears, no understanding, no
sense of humour, no faith. We need
prophets to get up in our pulpits and mock at
us.   We want saints who by abandoning
rank and wealth, and by living humble loving
lives, will hold up to derision our false gods.

With the " man in the street " it is not
words that count, but deeds.   It has always
been so.   He needs the symbolism of action.
It is not the words of Christ but His Cross
that makes men love Him.   It is not the Sermon on the Mount, but the spitting and the
scourging and the naked body exposed to
mockery and insult that makes men take Him
seriously.   So with His Body the Church, it

is not sermons which are going to win the souls of men, but the symbolizing of faith in action. The chaplain who descends from the first or second class of a liner to address the steerage does not have one-quarter the hearing that he would have if he travelled steerage. The steerage passengers know that he is the representative of the great Teacher of humility, and they feel that he is not living the gospel that he preaches. The army chaplain who lives at brigade headquarters, and ministers to such battalions as are in reserve or at rest, does not get half the hearing that he would have if the men had seen him sharing their privations, their dangers, their boredom, in the front line trenches. To the man in the street the religion of Christ is before everything else a religion of love and humility. The preacher who shows him these will be listened to with respect, however faltering his tongue, however faulty his

logic. It is the same with the Church as a
whole. The man in the street does not believe in the Church because he does not believe in her sincerity, and he does not believe
in her sincerity because he sees in her corporate life neither humility nor love, but only
the repetition of the same class pride,
party strife, prejudices, and divisions that he
sees in society as a whole.

I have written elsewhere of the men who
at this time of national danger have sunk
their differences, swallowed their pride, over-
come their prejudices, and enlisted in the
citizen army to fight with those whom for-
merly they despised and disliked, for a common ideal. In the army, men are learning
what poor things their pride and prejudices
were. They are learning the value of the
virtues which are common to all classes, the
fundamental virtues of courage and cheerful-
ness, and unselfishness, and honesty. They

are learning to love and honour men with whom in civil life they would have had no dealings. When the war is over it must be the care of the Church to show these men how in the fellowship of Christ's Body they may still use their diversities of gifts, in the same spirit of mutual respect and loyalty, and for the furtherance of a common ideal of life.

CHAPTER VIII

MISSIONS

THERE are few subjects about which the keen Churchman is more convinced and the average man more dubious than the necessity for and utility of foreign missions. The keen Churchman feels that it is one of the chief duties of the Church to spread the gospel until " the earth shall be full of the knowledge of the Lord as the waters cover the sea." The average man questions whether the Church is fit to preach till she has set her own house in order, and points to travellers' tales of the failure of missions as a proof that his scepticism is justified.

For both these views there is a certain amount of justification. On the one hand, it is a law of nature and of God that that which does not fulfil its destiny shall die. If the Church is not missionary she will die. On the other hand, it is indisputable that the success of missions is not what one would expect. Missionaries do an enormous amount of good in the way of education and medical relief; but the number of their converts, and the character of their converts, is disappointing, and so is their total effect on the life of the people among whom they work. Something is wrong with missionary methods.

Personally I can only speak from the point of view of a traveller in missionary countries (*e.g.* Madagascar, British East Africa, Mauritius, Ceylon)—a traveller who has wished to think well of missions, and has been at some pains to understand their difficulties, and to estimate their degree of success. Perhaps it may not be out of place for me to say, as a proof of my good will towards missions, that some six years ago I did actually volunteer for missionary service in Central Africa but was rejected on medical grounds.

Generally speaking, the charge against missions is that they make few converts and have a pernicious effect on those whom they influence. It is an old story that the mission boy is the biggest rascal to be found, far more dishonest than the unregenerate savage. Of course, I am talking chiefly of Africa. I honestly do not think that it is enough to answer that charge by a denial. It has appeared to me that a great many natives attend the mission schools, and even simulate conversion, for purposes of their own. They want to become servants, or in some fashion to be the go-between to the white man and the native, which is often a profitable occupation. Unfortunately, it is often not a very honest one. A native head-boy will often cheat the other boys of part of their wages, and deduct a percentage for himself when paying his master's bills. Native guides are generally rogues, and often pimps. In order to enter any of these lucrative and rather dishonest professions, the first essential is to learn English, and the easiest way to do that is often to attend the mission school. I have even known cases where natives have become priests in the English Church solely for mercenary reasons, and very unpleasant people they are. It would almost seem as though, in order to make real converts, it would be necessary to take precautions against its being worth while from the worldly point of view for natives to become converts.

A further very real difficulty of the present system is that as soon as a native becomes a Christian he ceases to be uncivilized, and becomes semi-civilized. He wears trousers and a jacket instead of a blanket and a coat of grease. A female wears petticoats and a blouse instead of the old short skirt which in European eyes is so immodest. It is hard to see how this can altogether be avoided, for undoubtedly in the case of unregenerate savages the introduction of Christianity is bound to revolutionize the whole social outlook. The Christian native can no longer buy a dozen wives, and amuse himself by hunting and fighting while his wives do the work. And I suppose that the modest attire of the white woman is only a symbol of the altered attitude of her menfolk towards her. Yet the effect often is to make the savage into a bad imitation of a white man, and to cause him to thank God that he is not as other men, which is a definitely unchristian frame of mind to be in. To say the truth, when the mission boy is not a rogue he is often something of a prig.

I fancy that if I were a savage I should regard the Christian life, not as a fuller, freer, nobler life than mine, but as a duller, more restricted kind of life, with certain compensations in the form of self-esteem and comfort and opportunities for making money.

I confess that with regard to some missions that I have come across I have found myself wondering whether after all they were teaching Christianity, or a kind of adapted English respectability which was not really a religious thing at all. I have heard the same sort of criticism made even by missionaries themselves of missions in India.

Perhaps we are not sufficiently clear ourselves about the real content of Christianity. Perhaps we confuse it in our minds with elements which, though associated with Christianity in England, are not really a part of Christianity at all. Perhaps we adopt a wrong attitude towards our black brethren.

Christianity, after all, is not a matter of clothes or of speech. It is possible to be a Christian and wear a blanket and be unable to speak a word even of pidgin-English. Brother black is probably a good deal less immodest than he looks, and possibly we are a good deal more prurient than he. Christianity will not change his colour or his climate or the shape of his skull, and so possibly we ought not to permit him to imitate us, but rather urge him to be his own best self, in a manner suited to the conditions of his existence. The two chief Christian virtues are, perhaps, humility and unselfishness, and I somehow fancy that these have been insufficiently insisted on in some missions.

I have not said anything about the wicked settlers or the district commissioners, whose unchristian example is so often alleged as a cause of the failure of missions, because I am quite sure that the less the missionary has to do with them, and the less he identifies himself with them, the better he will succeed. Generally the official is a good friend to the native. Often the settler is not. Neither is apt to favour the missionary. Unfortunately, at first the native is apt to lump all white men together, rather to the missionaries' dismay. But they must play their own game as independently as possible, and trust to time to set matters right. Nevertheless, it is a great advantage if the missionary can be first in the field. In the Hova country in the centre of Madagascar the missionary arrived first. After he had made a good deal of headway, he was expelled from the country, and the native Church was exposed to a severe persecution. The result is that in the Hova country one finds the nearest approach that I know of to a native Church racy of the soil. Every village seems to have its place of Christian worship. Tan-

anarive is full of churches of all denomina-
tions, and when I attended Holy Communion
in the cathedral I found myself in the midst
of a huge Hova congregation, listening to the
service in the native tongue, and felt as I
have never felt before or since the possibil-
ities of foreign missions. I believe that in
some measure the U.M.C.A. and the C.M.S.
in Uganda have also profited by being
first in the field, arriving in the country
with no protection, and depending for their
success almost wholly on the power of Christ
crucified.

I have not mentioned Christian disunion as
a source of failure, because I am convinced
that the real cause of failure lies much
deeper, and because I am also convinced that
organized co-operation is only a very small
step towards success. There is only one way
to win men to Christ, and that is to show to
them something of His love, and humility,

and quiet strength, and humorous common
sense, His distrust of the efficacy of human
aids to success, and His quiet confidence in
the power of love and truth.

There are, dotted about the world, many
poor missions, where men and women, often
lacking in tact and breadth of mind and education, toil year after year to win the heathen
by loving and humble service. They do not
succeed. They are often despised alike by
European travellers and by the natives themselves. Yet inasmuch as they are witnessing
in their lives to the truth that love and humility and purity are stronger than money and
organization and wisdom, I am convinced
that they are sowing a harvest which another
will reap. No one is such a vulgar, snobbish materialist as the native when he first
comes into contact with civilization. Civilization comes with arms full of glittering toys
for which the native reaches out both hands,

and for which he will submit to discipline, and sacrifice his most ancient customs and habits.   As yet he has no eyes for spiritual riches, yet their turn will come, and it is for the Church to witness to them meanwhile in humility and love and patience and faith.

This may sound inconclusive; but after all, is not our experience of home missions much the same?   It is easy enough to succeed in filling clubs, but much harder to fill churches. And the cause is often that the missionaries themselves have not a clear enough idea about where middle-class respectability ends and Christianity begins.   Too often the boys and men whom they convert show but one sign of their change of mind — a shame of their work and poverty and class and the genesis of a social ambition.   Too often the outward sign of conversion is a collar rather than unselfishness, and too often the collar is really the symbol of a new servitude rather than of a new liberty.

Perhaps this chapter is an impertinence. I have written it, not because I regard myself as an expert, but because I have tried to be a friendly critic. Six years ago at Oxford I joined a " Missionary Campaign," and stumped the country uttering perfervid denunciations of the critics of missions. I could not do that quite in the same way now. As a Churchman I feel that the hour of self-criticism and repentance should not pass us by without some thought of the failure of missions.

PRINTED IN THE UNITED STATES OF AMERICA

THE following pages contain advertisements of a few of the Macmillan books on kindred subjects.

A Theology for the Social Gospel

By WALTER RAUSCHENBUSCH

Author of "Christianity and the Social Crisis" and
"Christianizing the Social Order"

Cloth, 12mo, $1.50

This book, which embodies the Taylor Lectures given at Yale during Convocation Week in April, 1917, takes up the old doctrines of the Christian faith, such as Original Sin, The Atonement, Inspiration, The Sacraments, and shows how they can be re-interpreted from a modern social point of view and expanded in their scope so that they will make room for the salvation of society as well as for the salvation of individuals. The work is practical and inspiring and covers ground not previously traversed by writers.

THE MACMILLAN COMPANY
Publishers   64–66 Fifth Avenue   New York

Are You Human?

By WILLIAM DEWITT HYDE

50 cents

"Like a stinging fresh breeze laden with the very salt of life and vigor. . . . Every man in his young day ought to get and digest this book."— *Pacific Churchman.*

"A song of quick hope for the living."— *Oakland Tribune.*

"A vast amount of wisdom is compressed into small compass."— *Charleston News and Courier.*

"An admirable little gift to lay upon the table of every high school and college boy in the land."— *Unity.*

"Inspiring and encouraging thoughts presented in attention-arresting fashion for busy people."— *Nashville Banner.*

It's All in the Day's Work

By HENRY CHURCHILL KING

50 cents

"Good bracing counsel, such as the young men and women, at Oberlin or anywhere else may profit by, abounds in Dr. King's pages. It is a book for all who wish to acquit themselves well in the battle of life."— *The Dial.*

"A fine combination of the essay and the sermon, with none of the stilted style of the former, and with the directness of the latter, but better than either because of the sustained interest and the personal touch.

"It is a fresh, breezy, and brave appeal to face life as it is, and to make the best of it. It is only a little book, but it is a book for big men, whether sixteen or sixty."— *Universalist Leader.*

THE MACMILLAN COMPANY
Publishers   64–66 Fifth Avenue   New York

Why Men Pray

By DR. CHARLES L. SLATTERY,

Rector of Grace Church, New York

Cloth, 12mo, $1.00

Dr. Slattery's handling of his subject is fresh, unconventional, and remarkably liberal in tone; he writes with sympathy and deep religious insight of a question close to the thought of a great number of people. The theme is developed in a steadily climactic line toward the heights of spiritual thought, with frequent pertinent illustrations from personal experiences. The author is in the front rank of the younger men in the Episcopal Ministry; his book carries an authoritative and appreciative message to the steadily increasing number of people who find prayer of intimate and significant value in their daily lives.

"A little volume of unusual power and insight. . . . The meaning of prayer, its value and results in life and character are very practically and helpfully explained."— *Independent*.

THE MACMILLAN COMPANY

Publishers   64-66 Fifth Avenue   New York